IDEAS IN PSYCHOANALYSIS

Envy

Kate Barrows

Series editor: Ivan Ward

ICON BOOKS UK

TOTEM BOOKS USA

Published in the UK in 2002
by Icon Books Ltd., Grange Road,
Duxford, Cambridge CB2 4QF
E-mail: info@iconbooks.co.uk
www.iconbooks.co.uk

Published in the USA in 2002
by Totem Books
Inquiries to: Icon Books Ltd.,
Grange Road, Duxford
Cambridge CB2 4QF, UK

Sold in the UK, Europe, South Africa
and Asia by Faber and Faber Ltd.,
3 Queen Square, London WC1N 3AU
or their agents

Distributed to the trade in the USA
by National Book Network Inc.,
4720 Boston Way, Lanham,
Maryland 20706

Distributed in the UK, Europe,
South Africa and Asia by
Macmillan Distribution Ltd.,
Houndmills, Basingstoke RG21 6XS

Distributed in Canada by
Penguin Books Canada,
10 Alcorn Avenue, Suite 300,
Toronto, Ontario M4V 3B2

Published in Australia in 2002
by Allen & Unwin Pty. Ltd.,
PO Box 8500, 83 Alexander Street,
Crows Nest, NSW 2065

ISBN 1 84046 353 8

Series editor: Ivan Ward

Typesetting by Hands Fotoset

Printed and bound in the UK by
Cox & Wyman Ltd., Reading

Introduction

Envy was recognised as one of humanity's greatest problems long before the days of psychoanalysis. It is, after all, one of the seven deadly sins, and according to Chaucer it is 'the worst sinne that is. For, truly, all other sins are against one special virtue, but Envy is against all virtues and all goodnesses ... and that is like to the Devil that ever rejoiceth him in man's harm.'[1]

Chaucer says that envy is full of sorrow in another man's goodness and prosperity, but joyous in another man's misfortune. This is the unique feature of envy: its lack of any positive aim. All other 'sins' have an aim which, though it may be misguided or self-seeking, seeks to obtain an object of desire. Greed, avarice, lust, pride, all in their own ways may be driven by the wish for something desirable, albeit at someone else's expense. Only envy can lead to no gain, for the object of admiration is spoilt by the envy and thereby rendered undesirable. The only obvious gain would seem to be sadistic pleasure – 'joy of another man's harm'.[2]

Chaucer describes some of the ways in which envy makes its presence felt, and they will be familiar to all of us. He mentions 'bakbyting or detraccion' and describes someone praising his neighbour with a 'wikked intente; for he maketh alwey a "but" ate last ende that is worthy of moore blame than worth is al the praising'.[3] Someone works very hard and selflessly for a charity *but* she is rather a do-gooder. Someone else is an excellent pianist *but* he does play a bit too fast. Some friends have been very helpful *but* they are rather patronising.

Definitions of Envy

Before going further, I would like to make it clear that there are two quite different ways in which the word 'envy' is used. Chaucer uses it to refer to the destructive, spoiling force which attacks the very persons or qualities that the individual admires. This is the kind of envy that psychoanalysts also describe. However, the term is often used in common parlance to refer to a kind of envy that does not have this pernicious quality: instead, it consists in the painful pangs of an admiration that makes the individual aware of his (or her) own shortcomings. This second type of envy may lead to emulation or to acceptance of one's limitations rather than to spoiling and destructiveness. I envy you your good qualities, skills and beauty but this does not necessarily mean that I want to spoil them. In fact, my admiration of these attributes may inspire me to make better use of my own.

When the individual cannot hope to achieve that which he envies, he may still feel enriched by it and take something good from it. An older person envying the young may feel invigorated by their liveliness and optimism, even if his appreciation carries a painful edge of recognition of the fact that he can never again *be* young. Someone envying an artist or writer could not hope to acquire their talent and skill, but might feel inspired by their creativity and their view of the world.

Living with a certain amount of this type of envy is intrinsic to the appreciation of others and of what they have to offer. It has sometimes been called 'emulatory envy'. I will never become a brilliant musician, none the less I can be inspired by the qualities of the music and the emotions it conveys.

Living with the more destructive form of envy is much harder, but is also a part of the human condition. This may be why, although we might deplore some of the envious characters with which literature has provided us, we understand them and, in a way, they appeal to us. As well as perhaps provoking our sense of righteous indignation, as do Shakespeare's Iago or Satan in Milton's *Paradise Lost*, for instance, these characters also evoke our sympathy: we know what it is like to be them. Very often, the villains of literature inspire greater interest and understanding than the admirable objects of their envy and destructiveness, for there is a villain in every one of us. We may be familiar with our acceptable qualities, but literature can help us to accept aspects of our personalities that it can be very hard to bear on our own. Destructive envy is perhaps the feeling it is hardest to know about in oneself, for it is the only emotion that seemingly attacks goodness *because it is good*. In addition to this, the effect of envy is to undermine one's own goodness and capacities as well as those of the envied person.

Internal Effects of Envy

Milton, as well as Chaucer, attributed envy to the devil, for Satan personifies envy through his hatred both of God's creativity and power, and of Adam and Eve and their untarnished sexuality and love. Satan, having been cast out of Heaven for trying to overthrow God, finds his way to earth and spies Adam and Eve. He is overwhelmed with envy:

Sight hateful, sight tormenting! Thus these two
Imparadis'd in one another's arms
The happier Eden, shall enjoy their fill
Of bliss on bliss, while I to Hell am thrust.[4]

As we know, Satan then proceeds enviously to engineer the loss of their blissful state and their expulsion from the Garden of Eden. He punishes them and God for his own downfall, and Milton has described the state of intolerable anguish that followed Satan's envious attack on God and his exile from heaven:

Me miserable! Which way shall I fly
Infinite wrath and infinite despair?
Which way I fly is Hell; myself am Hell;
And in the lowest deep a lower deep
Sill threat'ing to devour me opens wide,
To which the Hell I suffer seems a Heav'n.[5]

Satan's insatiable greed and devouring envy are projected into the gaping mouth of Hell. The sensation of spiralling downwards out of control, of infinite depths of despair, can be the result of extreme envy, for internal good figures are attacked, leaving no support to prevent the individual from his downward fall.

A six-year-old girl who very much wanted to be good at drawing could not bear it that another girl in her class was clearly more talented and easily produced much better drawings than she did. One day when she found herself alone in the class, she ripped up the drawing that the talented youngster had left out to dry. Soon afterwards she had an overwhelming feeling of horror at what she had done, her sense of shame was enormous and she felt even more inadequate than before. Her relative lack of talent was now greatly compounded by a sense of guilt and hopelessness about being able to put things right.

When we attack the external object of our admiration, we also attack its representation inside our minds. This leaves us without inner support and our guilt about the attack affects our sense of worth. If the people and qualities that we value – our 'good objects', as psychoanalysts call them – are attacked inside us, this can lead to a feeling of inner destruction and wretchedness.

What is it, then, that led the six-year-old to tear up the picture or Satan to wage war on

God? Perhaps it is not just that the objects of their envy are perceived as good, or superior, but that their goodness makes the girl, or Satan, or any one of us at times feel inadequate in comparison. We may be unable to tolerate not being the best. So although goodness is being attacked, this may not just be out of a wanton desire to harm, but out of another motive: to destroy something or someone whose goodness is experienced in a way that makes us feel bad. Envy always involves a comparison – we envy that which we lack.

Envy and Jealousy

It is important to distinguish between envy and its companion jealousy, although the two are often closely interlinked and overlap. Jealousy implies that there is someone or something we want to possess. The motive is acquisition, the destructiveness is a means to an end. This was recognised in French law: a murder committed out of jealousy, known as a *crime passionel* (crime of passion), incurred a lesser sentence than a murder committed for any other reason. The rival was killed in the service of a passionate, albeit murderously possessive, love. But the destructive form of envy means that nothing can be spared: the object of our admiration must be spoilt so that neither we, nor they, nor anyone else can enjoy it.

The difficulty of distinguishing between jealousy and envy is clear in this rather touching story. A two-year-old was excited about the birth of his younger brother, and while the mother and newborn were in hospital, he cross-examined his father on the facts of life – how the baby came to be there, how it was made and how it had come out. The father did his best to explain these things kindly and gently to his son, who seemed satisfied. But a bit later the son had an enormous tantrum about wanting to be at the hospital. The father, thinking that his son was jealous of the new baby, asked him if he wanted to be with his mummy. The little boy exclaimed vehemently, 'No! I want to *be* the mummy!' Seeing his mother's pregnancy, hearing about the birth, had evoked the envy that was expressed in the tantrum, but it was overcome to some extent when he was able to share it with his father. This little boy's envy was manageable and bearable, though, and therefore different from the more pernicious variety of envy, which is much harder to modify.

The examples of the girl who destroyed the painting and the boy waiting for the birth of his new brother are the kinds of experiences that often happen in everyday life. The boy could express his feelings to his father who accepted his envy and frustration about not being the mother, and this made his feelings easier for him to bear. With his father's support, he was beginning to develop an *internal* figure who could enable him to have some sympathy for, and tolerance of, his envy. In contrast, the girl was not able to tell anyone until years later what she had done, and continued to feel bad and very alone about the experience.

Our internal worlds are created partly by our own feelings and partly by our experiences of others. An envious attack can leave us without internal support because we feel as though other people have become imbued with our negative feelings. The young girl felt she could not turn to anyone in the external world because *in her mind* the potentially helpful figures had become as hostile and attacking as she had been. She feared that they would 'tear a strip off her', just as she had torn the picture. In some situations it may be that the parents actually are harsh and punitive and that the child would have good reason not to confess. The difficulty can also come from within the child. However, it is very often a combination of the two.

The two children referred to in the examples show us about two very different kinds of conscience. The little boy was able to use his father to help him to develop a benign, or compassionate, conscience which sees how we feel but does not retaliate and so helps us to bear aggression or pain. For whatever reason, the little girl, in her guilty isolation, was at the mercy of a punitive and unforgiving conscience which, while it might help her to control her behaviour in future, resulted in her being unable to forgive herself for her envious feelings. We all have these two kinds of conscience – compassionate and unforgiving – and turn to them at different times. They are formed by a combination of our own feelings and the actual kindness or harshness of the people in our lives. Destructive envy is often accompanied by a persecutory conscience leading in turn to loneliness and feelings of alienation.

One way in which we can feel that we are not alone with our envy is through literature, which gives us the opportunity of exploring our deeper emotions, and the examples I include in this book illuminate the experience of envy for us. Another way in which people can find out about their envy, and learn to cope with it rather than letting it spoil things, is through undertaking psychoanalysis. What do psychoanalysts have to say about envy? From Sigmund Freud[6] onwards, many key figures in the psychoanalytic world have found that envy can constitute the greatest obstacle to the successful outcome of an analysis, and that coming to terms with this envy can be of fundamental importance to the patient's ultimate well-being and mental health.

Freud

In *Analysis Terminable and Interminable*, written towards the end of his life, Freud describes how the patient can refuse to accept help from the analyst. He suggests that this is due to the man's fear of passivity and to the woman's envy of the penis.

The rebellious overcompensation of the male produces one of the strongest transference-resistances. He refuses to subject himself to a father-substitute, or to feel indebted to him for anything, and consequently **he refuses to accept his recovery from the doctor.** *No analogous transference can arise from the female's wish for a penis, but it is the source of outbreaks of severe depression in her, owing to the conviction that* **the analysis will be of no use and that nothing can be done to help her.**[7] [my emphasis]

Though Freud's view is centred on the penis as a symbol of immense psychical potency and value, he has nevertheless pinpointed a central clinical problem associated with envy: by definition, the envious person cannot accept help because he or she cannot bear to be given anything. The difficulty in both sexes is that of being able to accept things from someone else.

It would not be possible to give an account of the development of psychoanalytic ideas about envy without at least a brief mention of one of Freud's most contentious and fiercely debated contributions to psychoanalytic theory: 'penis-envy'. He asserted that children know of only one genital, the penis. In his view, the little girl saw herself as lacking a penis, or even as a castrated boy, rather than as having something in her own right. He thought that her envy of the penis could lead to later difficulties in accepting it in a sexual relationship.

While many analysts would agree that there

is penis envy in both sexes – after all, the little boy can envy the father's developed penis – the notion of the primacy of the penis has been strongly contested. As I shall go on to describe, the idea of childhood envy has been extended to include envy of the mother, in the first instance of the feeding breast. The concept has also been developed more fully to include an emphasis on the unique *functions* of the envied organ, or of the envied parent. The penis is therefore envied for its potency, the breast for its feeding capacity, the mother's body for being able to contain babies and both parents for being, in their different ways, sources of life.

Feminists have argued that it is the privileges of men in society that are envied, rather than the penis as such. Equally, the biological and societal privileges of women who give birth to their babies and feed and nurture them increase men's envy of women. For it is *difference* that arouses envy, especially if the difference is one upon which we depend.

Abraham

The psychoanalyst Karl Abraham (1877–1925) was to suggest that envy can cause difficulties at an earlier stage, drawing attention to the possibility of the infant's envy of the breast.

Like Freud, Abraham placed a lot of emphasis on the relationship to the father. But he also introduced ideas that were to change the face of psychoanalysis and were to be developed by subsequent analysts, in particular by his patient, Melanie Klein (1882–1960), a pioneer in adult and child psychoanalysis.

Abraham suggested that the infant may find it very hard to accept the fruitfulness of the breast, as well as the potency of the father. He pointed out that 'we must bear in mind that the pleasure of the sucking period is to a great extent **a pleasure in taking, in being given something**' [my emphasis].[8] He described how envy in the feeding relationship can interfere with the baby's enjoyment of being fed and can lead to a pattern of unsatisfactory relationships in which the individual cannot take things in from other people.

It was a new development in psychoanalysis to suggest that envy is already at work at this early stage. Abraham saw optimism and the ability to enjoy life as stemming from a satisfactory feeding relationship. But when this relationship goes awry and the individual cannot appreciate what he is given, things can become much more complicated. Abraham described a type of patient who cannot bear to take in what the analyst can offer him or her.

In place of making a transference these patients tend to identify themselves with the physician. Instead of coming into closer relation to him they put themselves in his place. They adopt his interests and like to occupy themselves with psycho-analysis as a science, instead of allowing it to act on them as a method of treatment. **They tend to exchange parts,** *just as a child does when it plays at being father. They instruct the physician by giving him their opinion of their own neurosis, which they consider a particularly interesting one, and they imagine that science will be especially enriched by their analysis ... In particular, they desire to surpass their physician, and to depreciate his psycho-analytical talents and achievements. They claim to be able to 'do it better'.... The presence of an element of* **envy** *is unmistakeable in all this.*[9] [my emphasis]

The observation that the patient 'exchanges parts' with the analyst is a startlingly simple account of the mechanism that later became known as 'projective identification'. In this manoeuvre the individual takes over the envied qualities of the other person, and projects his unwanted feelings into that person. The child puts himself above his father, standing on a high piece of furniture, for instance, and declaiming to the actual father how small and ignorant he is. Abraham, with the humorous touch that makes his works so readable, described an obsessional neurotic who for some months clung to the idea that he knew more about psychoanalysis than Abraham. Eventually he had the good grace to comment, 'I am now beginning to see that you know something about obsessional neurosis'![10]

Klein

Towards the end of her life Klein, like Freud, became convinced of the ubiquity of envy and wrote about it in her influential essay 'Envy and Gratitude'. She saw envy as a manifestation of the death instinct, a concept that has been a subject of lively controversy among psychoanalysts. Whether one thinks that there is a death instinct *per se*, or simply that there are destructive forces in human nature, envy is clearly an expression of these forces. This is because of its attack on goodness, and therefore on life itself. Klein went to the heart of the matter: 'The capacity to give and to preserve life is felt as the greatest gift and therefore creativeness becomes the deepest cause for envy.'[11] She saw envy as being directed at the mother as a source of life and sustenance, qualities of mind being envied as well as physical capacities.

Klein suggested that another person's peace of mind can give rise to envy. She describes how the patient's 'unhappiness and the pain and conflicts he goes through are contrasted with what he feels to be the analyst's peace of mind – actually his sanity – and this is a particular cause for envy'.[12]

A patient in analysis came to a session complaining that what she most wanted and most lacked was 'a peaceful mind'. She then proceeded to criticise in a carping, envious tone of voice a number of people who were helping her, and it became clear that she did not want them, or her analyst, to have peaceful minds, but to worry about all they might be doing wrong. When, through analysis, she came to see that it was her difficulty in accepting help and in living and letting live that was causing her lack of satisfaction, she did gradually become happier and manage to let go of some of her grievances.

Klein, like Abraham, thought that the earliest dependent relationship, to the mother and to the breast or bottle, is the first relationship in which envy plays a part. She put forward the hypothesis that

... the primal good object, the mother's breast,

forms the core of the ego and vitally contributes to its growth.... the whole of [the baby's] instinctual desires and his unconscious phantasies imbue the breast with qualities going far beyond the actual nourishment it affords ... [and] so enrich the primal object that it remains the foundation for hope, trust, and belief in goodness.[13]

To build on this foundation entails emotional work. Klein postulated that the baby initially splits his feelings into good and bad, idealised and persecutory. Babies can oscillate between states of blissful contentment and extreme distress and rage, and we consider this to be normal.[14]

Gradually, as a result of the mother taking in the baby's extreme feelings and helping him to bear them, his positive and negative feelings do not have to be kept so far apart. The baby comes to realise that the mother he hates is also the one he loves, and he develops a capacity to tolerate feelings of ambivalence. If these early stages are too interfered with by envy, the idealised and then the good object cannot be established in the baby's psyche and he becomes confused between good and bad. Klein suggested that this can form the basis for confusional states. (This was explored later in more detail by Herbert Rosenfeld.[15]) The baby – or later the child and adult – may also suffer from feeding difficulties if in his imagination he feels he has attacked the envied breast and made it become poisonous. Later, such early phantasies can result in difficulties in trusting people. Likewise, in an analysis,

... envy, and the attitudes it gives rise to, interfere with the gradual building up of a good object in the transference situation. If at the earliest stage the good food and the primal good object could not be accepted and

assimilated, this is repeated in the transference and the course of the analysis is impaired.[16]

In other words, the patient experiences difficulty in digesting and assimilating the insight the analysis makes available to him.

An example from an analysis may illustrate the connection between concrete disturbances in relation to the breast and symbolic disturbances in relation to creativity and fulfilment. A young woman who sought analysis with a severe eating disorder and a social phobia nevertheless felt that her greatest problem was her difficulty in maintaining an interest in life. She had the self-awareness to realise that it was not her lack of wealth or possessions, not even physical health that troubled her most of all, it was her difficulty in sustaining a live interest in people and in what the world had to offer her.

This problem turned out to be linked to the

eating difficulties and the phobia, because her suspicion of food and of people came from the same source. Her primary relationship to the source of food and of interest and creativity had been damaged by feelings of envy, so that she could not hold on to an internal good object as a basis for trust in either sources of nourishment or sources of human contact and interest.

However, the fact that she held on to a desire for interest in life was an enormous help to her. It provided the motivation for change, and helped her to be able to emerge from her withdrawn state and engage with life. This entailed having to deal in her analysis with an envious part of herself that undermined her own capacity for interest and enjoyment and attacked her analyst's capacity to help her. As she became more able to sustain her interest and involvement, she also felt grateful for her analysis and for life itself.

It might be asked, 'Why should anyone

attack their *own* capacities?' But it has to be remembered that it is impossible to attack the person who has what one wants without also attacking one's ability to relate to that person and to receive from him or her – and these are important capacities. The baby who has to wait for a feed and then turns away from the breast, the child who is angry with the mother for attending to others or even to herself, therefore feels that what she offers him is no good. This also undermines his own loving feelings and his capacity to enjoy and to feel grateful for what the mother is able to give.

Klein wrote with compassion about the vicissitudes of envy and the importance of gratitude, love and enjoyment in counteracting its damaging effects. She described how, if the baby has enough thoroughly satisfying experiences in the first few months, a basis of gratitude can develop that can serve to mitigate envy and destructiveness. Then an internal good figure becomes established 'which loves and protects the self and is loved and protected by the self'.[17]

Envy in Childhood

The emotions that arise in relation to the breast and the mother are also then experienced in relation to the father, the parents as a couple and their other babies, actual or imagined. Each new relationship can provide an opportunity for early feelings to be worked through again, in a different way and with a different person, so that while certain propensities are established in the first relationship, there are opportunities for development. The different relationship provided by the father can sometimes make it possible to experience envy in a less intense way than in relation to the mother, or the father may provide support in dealing with envious feelings. This was the case with the little boy described earlier who wanted to be his mother when she had just had a new baby.

However, it is not only the mother and father who are envied, it is also the link between them. When the baby begins to recognise that the parents have their own, different, relationship he is likely to experience a range of emotions: he may feel interested, excited and reassured by the fact that life goes on independently of him. Babies and toddlers often play happily if there is conversation going on around them. But at times they will also feel envious and jealous, and resent the fact that each parent does not exist exclusively for them. It is a common experience at a certain stage in a baby's or toddler's development for the parents' conversations to be shouted down and interrupted by a youngster who wants to be in the middle.

Likewise, sleeping difficulties and the wish to get between the parents in bed can stem from the child's envy of the parents' sexual relationship, for even though the child may not be aware of sex in adult terms, he will be aware of an exciting and important aspect of the relationship from which he is excluded and he may wish to spoil their chances of pursuing this private relationship.

Although envy is evident even in these first relationships, it can also rear its head in new situations and re-evoke earlier conflicts. I have emphasised how envy is most evident in a dependent relationship. It can also be evoked by change, which can bring out our insecurities and our feelings that someone else has got a better deal. In particular, new phases in development can usher in envious feelings: weaning, a new baby, going to school and leaving home may all provoke jealousy and envy about what is being given up and the fact that someone else, in fact or in phantasy, now occupies the previous position. We have to

33

realise anew that the world does not revolve around us, that in fact the breast or mother, the situation from which we are moving away, can manage perfectly well without us and is an independent source of nourishment and support – to someone else. There may also be envy about those who are well established and more successful in the new stage.

The more satisfied the individual has been during the previous stage, the better chance there is of managing to let go, and of moving on to the next stage without too much rancour. But if there has been little satisfaction, then it will be harder to let go of the prerogatives of one stage and move on to the next. The child may protest at learning to walk, for this means not having to be carried any more, or at learning to talk, because this means more clearly having a separate mind from the mother. If envy is excessive, then the experience of development can become soured and grievance wins the day. Moaning and whingeing can sometimes mask envy of the mother who is not exclusively devoted to the child and jealousy of others who have her attention. In these situations, envy is closely interwoven with jealousy, but the amount of bitterness or rancour may give us a clue about how much envy underlies the complaints.

Sometimes envy can be masked when the infant, or the infant-part of the adult, feels that he controls the source of nourishment, so that he avoids acknowledging that there is a separate source. The child or adult who repeats some new insight or information that he has just been given as though he had thought of it all by himself may be similar to the baby who feels that he controls the breast.

Envy in Adolescence

Adolescence is a stage when envy is likely to be acute, for the adolescent has to cope with insecurity and uncertainty about the future and about his (or her) own developing identity. Professional work and sexual relationships, until this point the prerogative of adults, may now be attainable and yet may take time to attain. He may envy those who have an idea of what they want to do in life and who have the means or capacities to achieve it. He may envy those who have work, or good exam results, or those who have a secure sexual relationship. Now, what he makes of his life is more clearly up to him than ever before, and the prospect can be frightening. At the most extreme, he may withdraw into nihilism about adult values, work and relationships, and this can be an expression of envy of things that seem too hard to manage. He may refuse to study, to get a job, to help in the house, turning away from what is on offer, feeling that it is unbearable not to have the perceived achievements of adulthood straight away.

Adolescents are expert at making each other feel envious. Girls, and increasingly boys, will use their clothes and looks to project envy into their peers, and will hope to appear enviably 'cool'. To be 'cool' is to give the impression of not being anxious, of being unaffected by the anxieties and turbulence of their peers and, of course, of themselves. So the envy that is projected is envy of a trouble-free state of mind, a state of mind in which the adolescent would not find himself in the inevitable turmoil of his youth. Adolescent envy is often bound up with insecurity and is common currency. It is not always a permanent personality trait and can diminish as the adolescent gradually becomes more secure in himself. However, in cases where envy has been a serious problem in infancy and early childhood, its hold on the adolescent will be more powerful.

A young woman who had deeply envied her mother as a small child had attempted to deal with the envy through being very competitive and successful and projecting her envy into her younger siblings. In adolescence, she could not keep up the pace, and dropped out, running away from home and school and undermining any attempts to help her. She became promiscuous and despairing of herself and her prospects. She had come up against the envy of adult achievement and sexuality that she had denied for so long and it led her to flee from the very things she might want to achieve. She eventually found her way to psychoanalysis and managed to face the debilitating envy that had been preventing her from getting on with her life.

Envy in Adult Life

In adult life as in childhood and adolescence, if envy has got out of control at an early stage, it will reassert itself in times of stress and need to be worked through again if creative and positive feelings are to gain the day. Times of stress include both hard times (such as illness or misfortune) and times of change or challenge.

A patient applying for a job in a new organisation dreamt that he had a scar on his shoulder where a bit had been chiselled out, and this was now overlaid by a new scar of the same kind. He said that this dream reminded him of how he used to deal with new situations (such as moving to a new school) by having a 'chip on his shoulder' rather than recognising that there was a group of people whom he could like and want to be accepted by. This patient had been very put out by the births of his younger siblings – the first 'new group of people' in his life – and his early feelings of envy and jealousy were revived in new situations. He had dealt with the births of these younger siblings by becoming aloof and unapproachable, by having a chip on his shoulder.

New situations do revive old scars and old feelings that need to be worked through again. However, the new experiences can also provide the possibility of change and of the earlier, raw feelings becoming more bearable. In the case of the man with the chip on his shoulder, he was able to use psychoanalytic insight to enable him to become more communicative and to give and take more in his work and relationships.

When early experiences have been dominated by envy it will be re-evoked at later stages of change. As people get older, there is bound to be some envy of the younger generation and the future that they have ahead of them. These pangs of envy and of loss can be compensated for by pleasure in the lives of others and gratitude for the life that the older person has had. However, if the envy is too great, it may lead for instance to condemnation of 'the youth of today' – envy disguised as disapproval.

Milton wrote of 'Time, the subtle thief of youth',[18] and the ravages of time may indeed be experienced as an envious theft. When some old people start to become senile they will be convinced that things are being stolen from them – their money or their beloved possessions, for instance. This may at times be a concrete expression of their feelings that their faculties and their inner wealth, the valuable things they have inside them, so to speak, are being stolen from them by someone who envies them their psychic riches and capacities. In old age the personality tends to fragment if there is much loss of memory and other mental capacities, and the envy may then be experienced concretely as coming from outside.

Envy is an emotion that it is painful to be aware of at any age and we often try to disown it. One of the most powerful ways of trying to get rid of it is Abraham's 'exchanging parts'. This was later described by Klein as projective identification and has become one of the central concepts of contemporary psychoanalysis, extensively written about and discussed. It is a way of getting rid of our unwanted feelings and trying to take over the feelings that we do want to have. If envy is the feeling we want to get rid of, for instance, instead of feeling envious ourselves, we project envy into the other person, subtly emphasising his (or her) inadequacies and hinting at our supposedly superior resources. We put ourselves in his smart shoes, and try to get him to wear our shabby ones, our feeling of inadequacy.

The little girl who becomes a 'little madam' usually has some inferior role for her playmate to occupy. The know-it-all culture buff may well make us feel ignorant and a philistine. Feelings of envy are got rid of, but the envied qualities that have been colonised as part of the exchange are tarnished in the process: a good mother is supplanted by a little madam, or a creative thinker by a know-it-all. The element of caricature often gives the game away, and shows the nature of the envy behind it, for the admirable, envied qualities have become less admirable and have acquired an unpleasant character. Sometimes there may be a grain of truth in an aspect of the caricature, for envy can be clever at spotting weaknesses and magnifying them, to the detriment of the whole person or the quality that is admired.

As this process is often unconscious, the individual can feel extremely uncomfortable if he comes to realise what he has been doing, and reclaims the envy he has been busy disowning. However, there are also some people who are well aware of feeling envious and who seem to lack the capacity for remorse about their envious attacks. They are, of course, much harder to deal with, as they seem incapable of the guilt and compassion that might lead to change, or at least to the desire to protect others from their envy. Sometimes it turns out that the capacity for remorse and concern has been projected into other people, such as relatives or people in authority. In other cases it seems as though the possibility of feeling concern has been stifled at its inception. Such people include the ruthless psychopaths or abusers who are unable to feel compassion for their victims. They manipulate the feelings of others to destroy their lives.

Iago

One notable literary villain of this kind is Iago in Shakespeare's *Othello*.[19] Iago is driven by his relentless envy of Othello, the Moor, and Othello's new wife, Desdemona. They have married in secret as Desdemona's father would not have given permission for this mixed-race marriage, though it is a marriage of mutual love and respect. Iago has other grievances too: the promotion of Cassio over him to become Othello's Lieutenant, and his resentment at no longer receiving money from Rodrigo who had been paying him to be the go-between for himself and Desdemona, now patently unavailable. He also has a (probably unfounded) suspicion that Othello has had an affair with his own wife, Emilia. Rather than taking steps to find out whether his suspicion is true or false, he determines to

... put the Moor
At least into a jealousy so strong
That judgement cannot cure ... (II, i, 299–301)

Iago projects his own jealousy and lack of judgement, his incapacity to test reality, into Othello and he seems to have no interest in the truth: he is exploiting his own and Othello's feelings for the purpose of manipulation, to bring about Othello's downfall. He engineers

Othello's unbridled jealousy in the service of
his own envy and plans to:

Make the Moor thank me, love me,
  and reward me
For making him egregiously an ass,
And practising upon his peace and quiet
Even to madness. (II, i, 307–10)

This is Iago's strategy to 'exchange parts',[20]
to get rid of his own feeling of being made
a fool of and to make Othello look up to
him. He will be in Othello's shoes, not like
Macbeth who literally wants to become the
king, but in terms of being seen as 'faithful'
and 'honest' while Othello will go mad with
jealousy. Othello's peace of mind will be
forever ruined, as the latter realises when he
exclaims:

O, now, for ever

Farewell the tranquil mind, farewell content,
(III, iii, 352–3)

Klein pointed out that one of the qualities most envied is peace of mind. Other enviable qualities are goodness and innocence – the absence of envy. Iago cannot bear these qualities in either Othello or Desdemona and his plans are founded upon the despoilment of Desdemona's goodness and innocence:

So will I turn her virtue into pitch,
And out of her own goodness make the net
That shall enmesh them all. (II, iii, 351–3)

Iago gets Cassio drunk so that he is demoted from his coveted new post of Lieutenant. Iago then suggests that Desdemona should plead with Othello for Cassio's reinstatement, which provides Iago with ample opportunity to weave a picture that will stir up Othello to believe in

Desdemona's infidelity. The plan is successful and Othello's mind is gradually poisoned with jealousy until he suffocates his wife then stabs himself. Unlike some of Shakespeare's other villains, Iago shows no remorse at any time, though Othello demonstrates heartbreaking sorrow for the ruination of his love:

O, Iago, the pity of it, Iago! (IV, i, 192)

Iago seems unmoved by such feelings and in this he seems to represent envy incarnate. He warns Othello:

O beware, my lord, of jealousy.
It is the green-eyed monster which doth mock
The meat it feeds on. (III, iii, 169–71)

It has been suggested that this is a more accurate description of envy than of jealousy, and that the two terms were used more interchangeably in Shakespeare's day, jealousy being a much more commonly used term than envy. The 'green-eyed monster' is certainly Iago, for his mockery knows no bounds. Particularly in the realm of sexual insults, Iago's scorn and lewdness are designed to shock, suggesting that it is the loving sexual relationship that is abhorrent to him. He says to Brabantio, Desdemona's father, informing him of Desdemona and Othello's secret marriage:

Even now, now, very now, an old black ram
Is tupping your white ewe. (I, i, 88–9)

... you'll have your daughter covered with a Barbary horse, you'll have your nephews neigh to you, you'll have coursers for cousins ... (I, i, 113–15)

Iago attacks the loving sexuality of the couple,

making it into something obscene and crude, and he mocks the future progeny of the intercourse. Professor of English Literature Frank Kermode has pointed out how 'Iago's interest in sex is to watch others doing it, or at least to think about them doing it'.[21] This kind of voyeurism also changes the nature of the sexuality: 'Iago naturally has no use for the language of courtship; all love-making for him is merely the submission of the will to the base passions of the body. He assumes that Othello is a "lusty Moor" [II, i, 294].'[22] His racism and crude sexual language suggest the projection of forbidden sexuality, which is envied and then attacked. He breaks up the couple's wedding night and later works on Othello to get him to see Desdemona in the same debased way as he does, exulting in his success:

The Moor already changes with my poison.
Dangerous conceits are in their natures poisons,

Which at the first are scarce found to distaste,
But, with a little act upon the blood,
Burn like the mines of sulphur.... Not poppy,
* nor mandragora*
Nor all the drowsy syrups of the world,
Shall ever medicine thee to that sweet sleep
Which thou owedst yesterday. (III, iii, 331–7)

Iago is an expert in manipulative envy: he knows exactly how to ensnare his enemy and he does it remorselessly. He supplants his knowledge of the sexuality of the couple and the thought of their progeny with his own monstrous conception:

I ha't. It is ingendered. Hell and night
Must bring this monstrous birth to the world's
* light.* (I, iii, 395–6)

The warped conception and monstrous birth of Iago's plot to make Othello destroy Desdemona and himself shows the manipulative power of an envy whose aim is devastation. Iago knows he will gain nothing from his plans except the triumph of destruction. But he has controlled events and ruined what he felt excluded from as though to deal with his feeling of envy through the annihilation of those he envied.

Iago's consuming hatred of untarnished sexuality, and of emotional innocence, freedom from envy, resembles the hatred that can be found in some forms of sexual perversion. In child abuse there can be an element of envy of the child's innocence, which of course is forever ruined by the abuse. In transvestism the mockery can be ferocious, feminine attributes, for instance, being supplanted by a garish or grotesque take-off of femininity.

A respectable married male patient had been very prone to mockery of people whom he might otherwise respect, finding it hard to recognise what others had to offer. He brought the following dream: *He was in an art exhibition and really appreciating the detailed work of a female artist. He recognised how much time and care it must have taken her to produce such good work, which was both moving and well executed. Suddenly he noticed a transvestite, dressed in a ridiculous fashion as a woman, who was twirling around, creating quite a stir and taking the attention of the people in the gallery away from the paintings.*

The patient felt distracted and confused and woke up. He thought that in admiring the paintings done by the female painter and the hard work involved, he was appreciating his analysis and the work done by his female analyst. The transvestite figure excited and horrified him, and reminded him of a time in his youth when he dressed garishly to attract attention, though he had never been a transvestite. It seemed clear that this envious, attention-seeking aspect of him was in danger of taking him away from his developing capacity for appreciation.

Trying Not to Know About Envy

Very often envy will undermine good feelings without the envious person being aware of it. It is this hidden quality that can make envy so hard to manage and so subtly pernicious. It is experienced as the snake in the grass, the hidden enemy who infiltrates without being seen. We have many ways of protecting ourselves from knowing about our envy. The envy itself may be projected – for instance, when someone flaunts his (or her) possessions or attributes or busy life in such a way as to provoke envy.

A patient reacted to my telling her that I would (unusually) need to take a break in her analysis by informing me about a session that she also would be missing. She then went on to say how angry she was that some friends of hers had got in first with setting a date for a drinks party, which made the idea of giving such a party herself seem less exciting. It seemed that she experienced my telling her about my prospective absence as my 'getting in first' with my dates, as though I was giving a party that would put hers in the shade. The setting of dates seemed to provoke envy and competition, and a wish to get rid of the feeling of envy into me. Her birth had been followed by those of several siblings in quick succession. She felt that every time she began to settle down after the birth of the latest brother or sister, her mother announced the impending arrival of another baby, and her anger and envy were reignited.

If, however, we have projected our envy so successfully that we really are afraid of *being* envied, rather than flaunting what we have we may go to the opposite extreme and dumb ourselves down. We may dress down, or depreciate ourselves in other ways, so that no one would want to envy poor little us. Children often claim that they do not work for exams, that they aren't much good at things *really*, so that no one would want to attack them for working hard, or for what they achieve.

The fear of success is every bit as common as the fear of failure, for success can bring with it the fear of envy, real or imagined. Students seeking help as their final exams approach are just as likely to be afraid of success as they are of failure. Success often does lead in reality to being envied by other people: a first-class degree, getting a high-powered job, being singled out in any way can evoke envy in others. But if the fear of this envy is crippling, it suggests that it is compounded by our own projected feelings.

Another evasive manoeuvre is to project the responsible, concerned part of the personality on to others so that the individual feels no compunction about his envy. This can happen with teenage delinquency, where there may be envious attacks on property or life. The adults for a while carry the responsible part of the teenager, and hope to find ways to give it back so that he can again feel the sense of responsibility and guilt that would make him want to contain his feelings and care for the lives of others.

I have described the projection of envy on the one hand, and the projection of guilt and responsibility on the other. It is the bringing together of these two feelings, envy and guilt, that can be very painful. Sometimes it is so painful, or so feared, that the individual can harden his heart to avoid the pain or the feelings of despair about the damage done by his envious feelings. We may approach remorse, feel pangs of guilt, and then back off, feeling that there is too much damage to face. Then we split our feelings, getting rid of either the envy or the feelings of concern, so that we do not have to suffer the disturbing feeling of being aware of both.

Of course, we are often unaware that we have disowned our feelings in this way. In psychoanalysis, there can be an opportunity to reclaim aspects of ourselves that we have unwittingly disowned. As well as being painful, integrating unwanted aspects of the self can have a ring of truth which can feel more important than the pain of recognition. Klein describes the feeling of shock, when two parts of the self that had previously been kept apart come together. She suggests that this feeling of shock can be 'the result of an important step in the healing of the split between parts of the self'.[23]

Envy and the Psychoanalytic Relationship

A businesswoman in analysis had been struggling for some time with feelings of envy towards a colleague who had come into her department, bringing lots of new ideas and initiatives. The businesswoman realised that she had been avoiding her colleague because she did not want to be aware of how successful he was. She felt remorseful, and realised that she was also doing herself down, that she too had things to contribute. All this had great relevance to her analysis and was understood in terms of her relationship to her analyst as well as her colleague.

The businesswoman had previously felt that if she could get new insights from her analyst this put her in the shade, but she was beginning to feel that she too could have things to offer – it wasn't an 'either/or' situation. However, she came to her session after a party, describing how she had wanted to talk to her colleague, but a hostile woman kept interrupting. The hostile woman was aggressive to her colleague, as she is always aggressive to people who have more than she has or who have a lot to contribute. The patient seemed fascinated by this woman's aggression, and not at all bothered by the fact that she had driven her colleague away. She said that this woman always breaks up conversations.

In her analytic session it was possible for the businesswoman to see how her recent wish to be able to get more from her colleague and from her analyst was being undermined by a part of her that envied her capacity for a different kind of relationship, with more recognition of what the other could offer her and more awareness that her contribution too could be valued. When she realised that the hostile woman represented an aspect of herself she felt remorse, but this did also lead to a feeling of more genuine hope about being able to deal with the envious feelings that could so sabotage her more appreciative and constructive self. The obstructive woman could also be seen as a demanding child part of her who could not bear to be left out by a constructive couple, whether a mother/baby couple or a parental couple, represented by her new-found hopeful relationship with her analyst and her improved relationship with her colleague.

Envy often manifests itself in analysis in the form of a setback just when some progress has been made. This is so common that it has been called the 'negative therapeutic reaction'. The patient described above was reacting to having made some progress in her analysis; this progress threatened the envious part of her that did not want to feel dependent on her analysis or to recognise the difference that it made to her.

In many of the examples given above, the presence of envy seems clear. Often, however, it makes its presence felt in more insidious ways, gradually infecting the atmosphere. The analyst may come to feel that the analysis is not getting anywhere, that her work is not good enough, and she may come to realise that the sessions have been pervaded by an under-lying sense of futility. Over time it becomes clear that the patient does not want the analysis to be successful, or the analyst to have the pleasure of seeing the patient change. This slow poison is the subtle side of envy and the doubt it engenders is one of envy's hallmarks.

This is not to say that doubt is always caused by an infiltration of envy! The analyst can be at fault and always has to question where the problem lies. But the doubt engendered by envy is designed to make the analyst feel that she cannot trust herself or her own judgement. Her internal world is under covert attack, the envy being designed to destroy the very qualities the envious person might otherwise value and benefit from. Her judgement is under siege. Like Othello, she is up against the threat of an onslaught 'That judgement cannot cure' (*Othello*, II, i, 301). Only through becoming aware of this process can she help to move the analysis forward and regain access to the constructive part of the patient which has also been undermined.

Chronic doubt in one's judgement can be the result of an envious attack. In cases of borderline psychosis there may be an envious part of the personality, an envious internal figure who attacks the patient's judgement and ultimately his sense of reality. This attack on judgement is also experienced by the analyst.

An adolescent patient suffered from a persistent delusion that if he touched or even got close to certain objects he was going to catch germs that would lead to his death from an incurable illness. He was able to use insight about the connection between these 'germs' and his infectious feelings, but when he felt better and clearer in his mind as a result of this and other insights into his problem, he would suffer a relapse and his delusions would reassert their hold on him. There seemed to be a part of him that envied his own capacity to gain insight and to hold on to his sense of reality. This envious part of him resented the fact that his analyst could give him under-standing that could help him to get clear of his delusions. He also taxed the analyst's judge-ment about important analytic work that had been done.

The analyst was made to feel that perhaps it had been no use if it was followed by such severe deterioration, until she came to realise that the setbacks always followed helpful developments in the analysis. Envy that oper-ates at such a primitive level taxes patient and analyst alike, and this patient experienced it as a struggle between life and death, sanity and madness.

What Provokes Envy?

In dealing with envy in analysis as in other relationships there is an inevitable ebb and flow between the forces of creativity and life and those of envy and destructiveness. It is not always easy to see where those forces are located for there are always at least two people involved. Envy is much more likely to arise in certain kinds of relationships, which raises the question of how things are given as well as how they are received. If the giver enjoys giving and is not trying to make the recipient feel small, the latter may be able to accept what is offered with gratitude and with a wish to emulate and to give something in return. If, on the other hand, the giver does not seem to enjoy giving, or seems to be doing it to make himself (or herself) feel good rather than because he is really interested in the other person, then that person will feel injured and may feel envious: he is not being freely given to, so he cannot benefit from what is offered. It is important that the giver should be able to take pleasure in the recipient's enjoyment and feel interested in what he makes of the gift. If the giver cannot bear to take anything in return, then the gift will be harder to accept and is more likely to give rise to an envious response. (Elizabeth Bott Spillius has written about this aspect of envy.[24])

As we have seen, envy can be provoked unconsciously so it is always important to keep an open mind about what may be happening on both sides of the relationship in which it arises. Some of the examples I have given could be seen from different points of view: quite possibly the father who told his son about some of the details of procreation did excite his son's envy somewhat, or maybe the analyst who announced the date of her sudden absence did so in a slightly tantalising way. Perhaps Iago's envy was inflamed by Othello's insensitive treatment of him, and the almost too-good-to-be-true quality of his relationship with Desdemona.

If the giver is able to communicate that he doesn't see himself as perfect, the recipient is more likely to feel a spirit of common humanity that makes it easier to accept what is given and to deal with any envy that he does feel. This brings us to the question of envy and society.

Envy and Society

When thinking about society, it is essential, in particular, to distinguish between envy that is brought about by deprivation and inequality, and the envy described throughout much of this book which has to do with an intolerance of difference.

The term 'the politics of envy' has been used to justify huge inequalities in wealth and privilege, as though the underprivileged should manage not to be envious. Where there are gross inequalities there will be envy, but it can be caused more by deprivation than by inherent difficulties in tolerating the good fortune of others. For instance, some vandalism can be seen as a manifestation of envy which is provoked by the flagrant inequalities of society, rather than being simply a problem of the individual vandals and their destructiveness. There still remains the question of why some people turn to vandalism, others look for a job, and others try to change society.

The problem of envy in society involves interwoven personal and social factors. These are material and psychological: the teenage vandal may be out of a job and have no prospects of work or further education. Or he may be a disaffected boy who has had good educational opportunities but has felt himself to be part of a conveyer-belt education that has had no room for him as an individual, for what he might have to offer or for his limitations. There will also be the question of how inherently envious he is, and the factors contributing to this in his childhood and con- stitution. So the reasons for envious attacks on property can be as complex as society itself.

However, it is possible to see some forms of envious attack in society that do not seem to have anything to do with social injustice. Take Internet hackers, for instance. They are intelli- gent and clearly possessed of the skills and the computers that enable them to sabotage other peoples' communications. Their aim is to wreak havoc, in an arbitrary way, just for the sake of it. This seems like a much more destructive version of the child who wants to interrupt the parents' conversation. The hacker wants to damage the equipment so that no communication will be possible, and his pleasure comes from an envious spoiling and the satisfaction of beating the system.

The social manifestations of envy are by no means reserved for criminal activities. There are ways in which we collectively make use of envy in our society. Through the media and other institutions like the football clubs, music and film industries, we elevate celebrities to enviable positions of wealth and glamour, then attempt to destroy them with gossip and scandal and a denial of privacy – an envious intrusion into the lives that we have helped construct.

We allow advertisers to provoke our greed and desire for material goods, from fashion items to smart cars. It could be argued that advertising leads to emulation, but it does often seem to be a type of emulation that is based on a commercially produced dissatisfaction with ourselves and our image, an envious attack on our self-worth and our other values. This makes us tend to feel that we must buy something more to feel that we are of value, rather than appreciating what we have or holding on to our interest and involvement in what is beyond ourselves and our material possessions.

A woman in her thirties sought analysis because she was suffering from chronic dissatisfaction with life. She utilised a display of riches and glamour to provoke envy in others, but was deeply discontented and communicated a feeling of inner poverty. Any activity she thought of undertaking soon felt unappealing: social life seemed meaningless, sport was a waste of energy, reading was pointless. In using the trappings of wealth and fashion to project her envy, she was trying to get rid of it. But it was envy that made her unable to accept what life had to offer her in terms of interests and relationships. She seemed to have retreated from her intense feelings of envy and jealousy into a state of narcissistic withdrawal, in particular depriving others of the pleasure of being able to make her happy. When she became aware in her analysis that her disaffection with what life could offer was the result of her devaluing it *because* it had a lot to offer, she became less jaded in her attitude and began to appreciate her relationships and to develop wider interests.

Of course, not everyone makes use of wealth and possessions in this way, but it is all too easy to do so if you can afford it. Inequalities of wealth and opportunities within society and between societies are bound to provoke envy among the less fortunate individuals and societies, and guilt or denial among the fortunate. The widespread availability of television, with its commercially dominated programmes and advertisements, also exacerbates envy in areas where most commercial products are out of reach because of poverty.

One other social manifestation of envy that I would like to consider is the envy involved in discrimination against groups of people who are different from ourselves. The many divisions in our society can lend themselves to suspicion and mistrust. This brings us back to the type of destructive envy that is not only to do with deprivation or competition for resources, but also to do with the fact that it can be hard to accept what other people have to offer. It can be easier to denigrate a different group from our own and look for its faults than to open our minds to something new. Prejudice is largely based on the projection of unwanted feelings on to groups or individuals. We may attempt to disown our negative features, rather than being able to bear the fact that another group has some things we don't have, and accepting and enjoying the richness and variety of differ-ence.

In Conclusion

At this point, we might be advised to return to Chaucer: 'Certes, thane is love the medicine that casteth out the venym of Envye from mannes herte [heart].'[25]

Chaucer writes of the pain of acknowledging envy and attempting to make amends and suggests that it is the capacity to love that makes it possible to overcome envy. Manag-ing to acknowledge our envy and to care about its effects on our collective and individual lives is a manifestation of love, in that it can protect those who would otherwise be damaged by the envy. Or, where the damage has already been done, acknowledgement can lead to reparation and reconciliation. Insofar as we are able to take responsibility for our envy, a benign cycle can sometimes be set in motion, where bitterness and guilt can give way to enjoyment and gratitude, and to the realisation that the other person, or group of people, has been offering us something all along that we have been finding it hard to accept. Gratitude, the relief that it is possible after all to care for the other person, and enjoyment of what that person has to offer all serve to counteract the damaging effects of envy. It would be true to say that the bad thing about envy is that it attacks goodness; the good thing about coming to terms with envy is that this goodness can then be appreciated and enjoyed.

Acknowledgements

I would like to thank the following for their careful and imaginative reading of this manuscript: Paul Barrows, Ted Edgar, Caroline New, Jane Temperley and Ivan Ward. Thanks also to my patients.

Dedication

To my family

Notes

1. Chaucer, G., 'The Parson's Tale', in *The Canterbury Tales*, London: J.M. Dent & Sons Ltd., 1958, p. 561.

2. Ibid.

3. Ibid.

4. Milton, J., *Paradise Lost* (Book 4), London: Penguin Books, 1989, p. 92, lines 505–8.

5. Ibid., p. 80, lines 73–8.

6. Sigmund Freud (1856–1939) was the founder of psychoanalysis.

7. Freud, S., *Analysis Terminable and Interminable* (1937), in *The Standard Edition of the Complete Psychological Works of Sigmund Freud: Vol. XXIII*, London: The Hogarth Press and The Institute of Psycho-Analysis, 1953–73, p. 252.

8. Abraham, K., *Selected Papers on Psycho-analysis*, London: The Hogarth Press and The Institute of Psycho-Analysis, 1927, p. 397.

9. Ibid., pp. 306–7.

10. Ibid., p. 307.

11. Klein, M., *Envy and Gratitude and Other Works 1946–1963*, London: The Hogarth Press and The Institute of Psycho-Analysis, 1975, p. 202.

12. Ibid., p. 222.

13. Ibid., p. 180.

14. Emanuel, R., *Ideas in Psychoanalysis: Anxiety*, Cambridge: Icon Books, 2000, p. 23.

15. Rosenfeld, H., 'A Clinical Approach to the Psycho-analytic Theory of the Life and Death Instincts: An Investigation into Aggressive Aspects of Narcissism', in *The International Journal of Psycho-analysis*, vol. 52, 1971, pp. 169–78.

16. Klein, ibid., p. 185.

17. Ibid., p. 188.

18. Milton, J., 'On His Being Arrived to the Age of Twenty-Three', in *Selected Poems*, London: Constable and Company Ltd., 1993, p. 14.

19. Shakespeare, W., *The Tragedy of Othello, the Moor of Venice*, in *The Complete Oxford Shakespeare: Vol. III: Tragedies*, ed. S. Wells and G. Taylor, Oxford: Oxford University Press, 1987, pp. 1165–204.

20. Abraham, op. cit.

21. Kermode, F., *Shakespeare's Language*, London: Penguin Books, 2000, p. 176.

22. Ibid., p. 172. The reference to 'lusty Moor' comes from *Othello*, II, i, 294.

23. Klein, *Envy and Gratitude*, op. cit., p. 215.

24. Bott Spillius, E., 'Varieties of Envious Experience', in *The International Journal of Psycho-analysis*, 1993, vol. 74, part 6, pp. 1199–212.

25. Chaucer, op. cit., p. 564.

In case of difficulty in obtaining any Icon title through normal channels, books can be purchased through BOOKPOST.

Tel: +44 (0)1624 836000
Fax: +44 (0)1624 837033
e-mail: bookshop@enterprise.net
www.bookpost.co.uk

Please quote 'Ref: Faber' when placing your order.

If you require further assistance, please contact:
info@iconbooks.co.uk